EARTH

By ALFRED LEUTSCHER

Illustrations by JOHN BUTLER

METHUEN/WALKER BOOKS

Rich, poor, sticky, chalky or gritty; brown, red, white. All these words describe different kinds of earth. Seeds take root in earth and draw food from it. Grass, and weeds like groundsel can take hold even among cracks between bricks on buildings, where earth is hidden. Without plants, no animals – whether pigeons or us – can exist.

Clay is a heavy earth. After rain it is very sticky, squelching underfoot, making your boots muddy. The farmer's tractor leaves deep patterns in it. When clay is dry it becomes stiff and brittle. Red clay is used for making house bricks, roof tiles and pottery. The clay is baked hard in a very hot oven called a kiln. If you make mud pies you can bake them dry in the sun, though they will not be nearly as strong as kiln-baked clay.

Chalk is a soft white earth often found on sea cliffs. It is formed over millions of years from the shells of tiny, dead sea animals. Blackboard chalk is made from these tiny shells. If you are lucky, you could find ammonites buried in chalky rock. These are the fossils of an ancient sea animal which looked like an octopus covered by a curly shell. Thrift, or sea pink, grows on chalky earth by the seashore. On chalk hills you may see wild orchids.

Sand is loose, gritty earth. It stings your face and body when the wind blows behind it. Wind can whip sand up into hills, or dunes. In North Africa there are vast areas of barren desert sand. Palm-fringed oases provide the only water for animals like the camel and the desert fox.

Beach sand is made from pebbles, ground down by the ocean, then washed ashore to form beaches. Behind are dunes, piled high by the wind. This is where the natterjack toad lives, and where gulls lay their eggs. Marram grass, creeping across the dunes, helps hold the sand in place.

Earth made rich by humus is a world busy with wildlife. Humus is the rotted-down remains of dead leaves, plants and animals. This dark brown, fertile earth provides food and shelter for a huge number of worms, millipedes, slugs, snails and other soil animals. There may be three million earthworms in one big field. They, in turn, are food for a hungry blackbird or shrew. Worms make burrows that let in air and keep the humus fresh. Wood anemones thrive in this kind of soil.

When autumn leaves fall and decay they add more humus to the soil. In a forest of evergreens, however, there is little humus; the soil is poor and acid. The few pine needles that fall do not add much nourishment. The permanent gloom shelters deer and other shy animals, but blocks out life-giving sun and rain. Ferns, moss and autumn toadstools like the fly agaric thrive best. Seeds that drift from ripe pine cones will grow into new trees, unless a squirrel eats them first.

In mountainous places the land is snow-covered for much of the year. There seems to be no earth, but some flowers – such as white mountain avens and purple saxifrage – do grow here. Mosses and grass are eaten by hardy ibex. Mountain plants, called alpines, have long roots which reach down to find earth hidden deep between cracks and hollows in rocks. Inside mountains, water dissolves soft rocks such as limestone, and hollows out caves.

Many tropical forests flourish on rich, dark earth. Between the tall trees every space is filled with flowers and ferns. The parrot screams from a branch and the humming bird darts through the trees. An anteater searches for food below. But all these animals are in danger of extinction if the forest is cut down. Wind and water will then carry away the uncovered earth. Whatever soil is left the sun will burn hard and dry so that no plants can grow.

When animals and plants die, their remains are buried in the earth. Slowly, this earth becomes rock in which the hard parts of the plants and animals are preserved as fossils. The fossilized skeleton of a dinosaur reveals its size; its teeth tell us what it ate. Tyrannosaurus rex was a meat-eater; Anatosaurus ate plants. Fossilized plants found nearby show a dinosaur's habitat. We have also learned about past civilisations by digging into the earth.

Digging into the earth uncovers its riches:
coal, gold, diamonds and oil are some of
the valuable products we can find by digging
pit-shafts and oil wells. Deep below ground
the miner shovels coal, or cuts away gold-
bearing rock which is lifted to the surface.
Some of the oldest mines were dug by
Stone-age man for pieces of flint which
he made into tools and weapons.

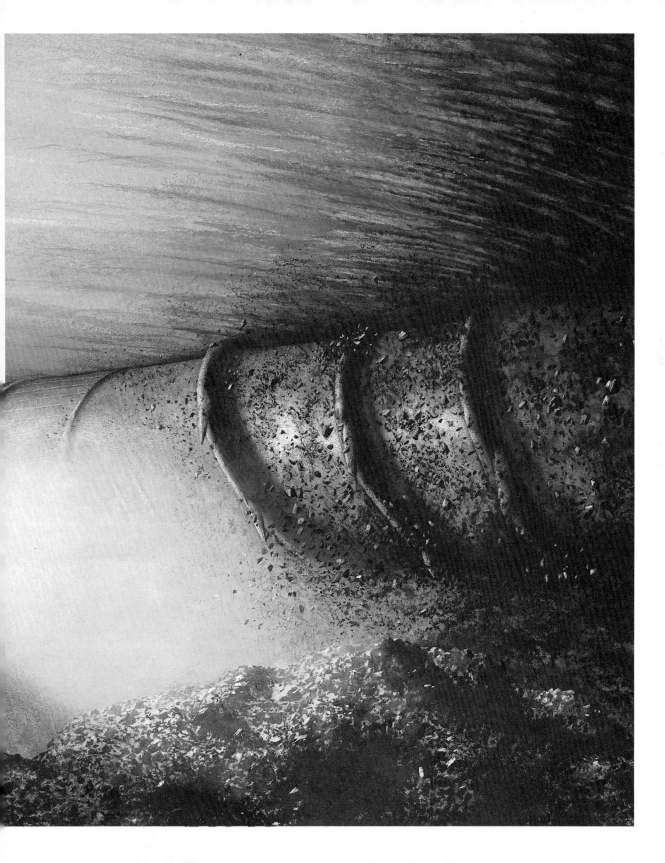

Earth is not always still and silent.
Suddenly, it may tremble. An earthquake
splits it open with a roar. Buildings
come tumbling down, trees are uprooted,
bridges collapse and railway lines buckle.
Volcanic eruptions also disturb the earth.
But the ash and lava volcanoes throw out
eventually make new, rich soil for farmers.

Farming began way back in the Stone Age, more than 7,000 years ago. Since then we have made increasing use of earth to grow crops such as wheat, potatoes, grass, rice and sugar. Farmers plough the soil before and after each crop to keep it clean. Some countries still use horses, oxen and even water buffalo, but in modern farming tractors pull machines which plough the earth. Sprays kill the weeds and fertilizers enrich the earth.